NATIONAL GEOGRAPHIC | **GLOBAL ISSUES**

M000200350

GLOBALIZATION

Andrew J. Milson, Ph.D.
Content Consultant
University of Texas at Arlington

Acknowledgments

Grateful acknowledgment is given to the authors, artists, photographers, museums, publishers, and agents for permission to reprint copyrighted material. Every effort has been made to secure the appropriate permission. If any omissions have been made or if corrections are required, please contact the Publisher.

Instructional Consultant: Christopher Johnson, Evanston, Illinois

Teacher Reviewer: Heather Rountree, Bedford Heights Elementary School, Bedford, Texas

Photographic Credits

Cover, Inside Front Cover, Title Page ©Justin Guariglia/Corbis. **3** (bg) ©Tommy Flynn/Photonica/Getty Images. **4** (bg) ©REUTERS/Rafiqur Rahman. **6** (bg) ©REUTERS/Beawiharta. **7** (tl) ©Steve Hix/Somos Images/Corbis. **8** (bg) Mapping Specialists. **10** (bg) ©AP Photo/Czarek Sokolowski. **11** (tl) Mapping Specialists. **12** (t) ©REUTERS/Peter Andrews. **14** (tr) ©Adam Warzawa/epa/Corbis. **15** (bg) ©Adam Warzawa/epa/Corbis. **16** (bg) ©Wang Dingchang/Xinhua Press/Corbis. **19** (bg) ©YM YIK/epa/Corbis. (br) ©Keren Su/China Span/Alamy. **20** (bg) ©Michael Christopher Brown/Corbis. **22** (bg) ©Chris Minihane/Alamy. **23** (tl) ©James Bedford. **24** (bg) ©Ken Banks/kiwanja.net. **27** (t) ©age fotostock/SuperStock. **28** (tr) ©David Engelhardt/Getty Images. **30** (tr) ©Scott Olson/Getty Images. (br) ©Lester Lefkowitz/Getty Images. **31** (bg) ©Tommy Flynn/Photonica/Getty Images. (br) Mapping Specialists. (bl) ©REUTERS/Beawiharta. (tr) ©David Sanger/David Sanger Photography/Alamy.

For permission to use material from this text or product, submit all requests online at www.cengage.com/permissions.

Further permissions questions can be emailed to permissionrequest@cengage.com.

Visit National Geographic Learning online at www.NGSP.com.

Visit our corporate website at www.cengage.com.

Printed in the USA.

RR Donnelley, Menasha, WI

ISBN: 978-07362-97523

14 15 16 17 18 19 20 21 22

10 9 8 7 6 5 4 3

CONNECTING THE GLOBE

Factory workers in Dhaka, the capital of Bangladesh, dry jeans after heavy rains. Jeans are one example of a global product.

HOW HAS GLOBALIZATION CHANGED THE WORLD?

Are you wearing blue jeans right now? You bought those jeans in the United States, but many people from around the world helped produce your jeans. Your jeans are a product of **globalization**—that is, the way countries use technology, communication, and transportation to connect with one another. Globalization connects governments, cultures, and **economies**, or systems of producing and distributing wealth. Globalization fuels trade and affects the way all of us live.

TRAVELING BLUE JEANS

The overall effect of globalization is to make it easier for people to make, buy, and sell goods. Take the jeans you're wearing, for example. The cotton came from the United States. In China, workers cleaned and dyed the cotton while factories in Malaysia spun the fibers into yarn. Workers in Thailand turned the yarn into fabric while others in a factory in Singapore cut the cloth. The zipper was made in Hong Kong; the buttons were made in Taiwan. Indonesians sewed everything together. Back in Singapore, workers attached labels and shipped the jeans to stores around the world.

Once all the parts of the jeans are ready, they are sewn together by factory workers in Jakarta, Indonesia.

These U.S. consumers are buying jeans made in countries all over the world.

MAKING THE WORLD GO 'ROUND

Globalization is nothing new; it has been around for centuries. Nearly 2,000 years ago, Europeans traded with China and other Asian countries along a route called the Silk Road. Merchants traveled in camel caravans along segments of the Silk Road to trade their goods. In exchange for valuable silk made by the Chinese, the Europeans sent gold, silver, and other goods to Asia. The trade caused each region to flourish.

Today, however, globalization is driven by new inventions, improved technologies, and countries that want to improve their economies.

WHAT IS THE IMPACT?

Globalization affects everyone in different ways. For many, globalization is a positive change. It brings people of different cultures together. It provides jobs for people in developing countries and gives them a way to make a living. It allows businesses to make products more inexpensively.

On the other hand, globalization often changes traditional ways of life. Languages may disappear and traditions may vanish. As people concentrate on producing more products faster, they sometimes ignore or replace old traditions. Millions can lose their jobs because the products they make can be produced less expensively somewhere else.

In some places, globalization widens the gap between rich and poor. It also can result in the misuse of **natural resources**, materials that come from the environment such as gold, coal, or oil. It can result in the mistreatment of a country's workers. While some individuals and countries prosper because of globalization, others struggle.

Explore the Issue

1. **Explain** What is globalization? Give two examples and explain why they are examples of globalization.

2. **Analyze Effects** What are two positive and two negative results of globalization?

Impact of Globa

Selected trade organizations

- European Union
- Asia-Pacific Economic Cooperation
- North American Free Trade Agreement and Asia-Pacific Economic Cooperation

UNITED STATES Globalization has caused many U.S. companies to move jobs overseas to save money. According to some, this has led to higher unemployment in the United Sates.

CASE STUDY 1

POLAND Globalization has helped Poland thrive; it is now the sixth largest economy in Europe. Low wages and loss of traditional farms have resulted.

NORTH
AMERICA

NORTH
PACIFIC
OCEAN

NORTH
ATLANTIC
OCEAN

SOUTH AMERICA Some believe that globalization is allowing foreign companies to use up the Amazon rain forest. Companies want to develop South America's other natural resources, including oil and gold.

SOUTH
AMERICA

SOUTH
PACIFIC
OCEAN

SOUTH
ATLANTIC
OCEAN

Explore the Issue

1. **Interpret Maps** Which trade organization does Poland belong to, and which does China belong to? What are the effects of globalization in each country?

2. **Draw Conclusions** How has globalization affected the poverty rate in India?

ization

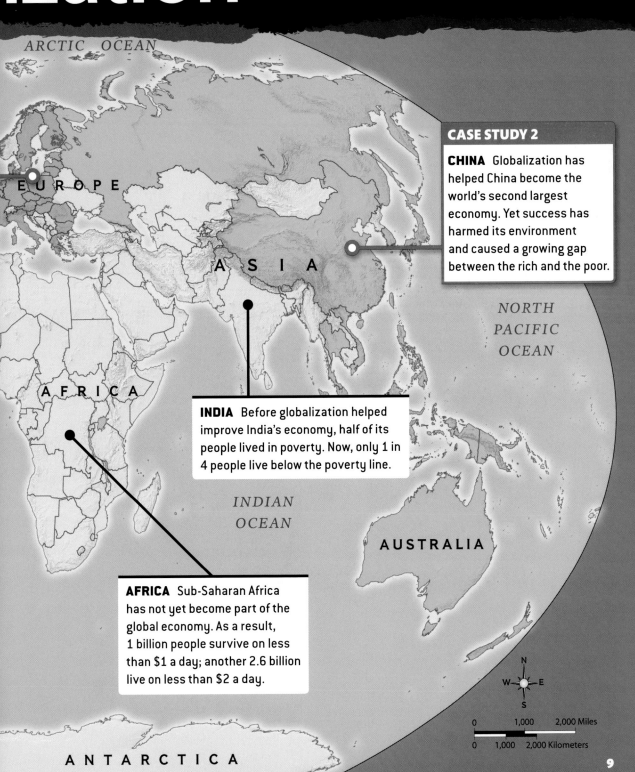

ARCTIC OCEAN

EUROPE

ASIA

AFRICA

NORTH PACIFIC OCEAN

CASE STUDY 2

CHINA Globalization has helped China become the world's second largest economy. Yet success has harmed its environment and caused a growing gap between the rich and the poor.

INDIA Before globalization helped improve India's economy, half of its people lived in poverty. Now, only 1 in 4 people live below the poverty line.

INDIAN OCEAN

AUSTRALIA

AFRICA Sub-Saharan Africa has not yet become part of the global economy. As a result, 1 billion people survive on less than $1 a day; another 2.6 billion live on less than $2 a day.

N
W E
S

| 0 | 1,000 | 2,000 Miles |
| 0 | 1,000 | 2,000 Kilometers |

ANTARCTICA

Poland
A NEW LAND
OF OPPORTUNITY

LOCATION! LOCATION!

Who would have guessed that a store that went broke in California would be very successful in Poland? Fernando and Magdalena Zucca had tried to sell Southeast Asian knickknacks in their California store since 1998. In 1999 they opened a store in Pozan, Poland. While their California store went out of business in the early 2000s, their new shop in Poland made a profit. The Zuccas could run their business much more cheaply in Poland. For the Zuccas and thousands of others, Poland has become a land of opportunity. By embracing globalization at the end of the 20th century, Poland arrived on the world economic stage.

European Union Countries

The European Union now has 27 member countries.

DEMOCRACY IN POLAND

Poland wasn't always prosperous. At the end of World War II (1945), **communists**, who believe in a classless society with no private property, ran the country. The state tightly controlled all businesses, properties, and other aspects of citizens' lives. That all changed in 1989 when communism collapsed and a **democratic** government, elected by the people, came to power. The government moved Poland toward **free enterprise**. This is an economic system in which private businesses organize and operate for profit competitively with a minimum of government interference.

At first the change strained Poland's economy. Prices skyrocketed and people lost their jobs. Then life slowly got better. In 2004, Poland joined the **European Union (EU)**, an economic and political association of European countries. The European Union developed from the European Economic Community, also known as the **Common Market**. This was an alliance that European countries formed in 1957 to drop trade barriers between members. The EU created a common currency, the euro, instead of each country having its own type of cash money. The EU became a major market that exports goods to the rest of the world. The same EU provided money and support to build Poland's new economy.

Poland's growing economy has led to new developments, such as this shopping center in Warsaw, Poland. The massive roof covers 10,000 square yards.

EXTREME MAKEOVER

In Poland, overflowing supermarket shelves soon replaced the dreary government-owned stores, where bread and eggs had always been in short supply. Shopping malls opened with American-style boutiques and fast-food restaurants.

Poland can thank the rest of the world, especially its European neighbors, for its extreme makeover. It became so cheap to run a business in Poland that foreigners invested money in these businesses. Some 350 American corporations, including beverage companies and computer makers, opened factories and employed thousands of Polish workers. European tourists flocked to Poland's cities, spending their money in hotels, stores, and restaurants. After it joined the European Union, Poland became one of the largest economies in the world.

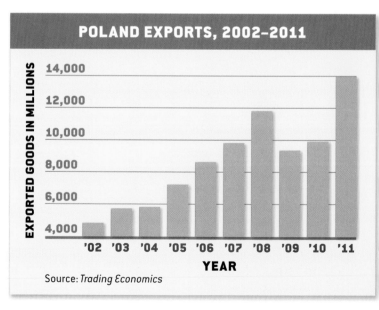

POLAND EXPORTS, 2002–2011

Source: *Trading Economics*

Wheat is loaded onto a modern well-equipped truck as corporate-run farms replace small family farms in Poland.

LOST JOBS AND TRADITIONS

What has this success cost Poland? Globalization caused many problems. In 2004 many workers left for better-paying jobs and education in other countries. Eventually unemployment increased. Many of those who couldn't find work received government benefits, putting Poland deeply into debt. The job situation got so bad in southwest Poland that out-of-work miners illegally reopened old coal mines. Many died digging the mines.

Even traditional farmers felt the pain brought on by globalization. Once Poland joined the European Union, people had to obey a new set of rules. Those rules made businesses, including farms, more productive, but presented farmers with new challenges.

For smaller farmers, such as Szczepan (SEH-puhn) Master, the new rules included building concrete floors in barns and buying special equipment to slaughter animals. Farms that could not afford the improvements went out of business. They were replaced by large, corporate-run farms. "It is impossible for me to farm," Master says. His words echo those of many small farmers in Poland.

NEW OPPORTUNITIES

Despite these problems, Poland's newfound wealth changed the way people live—for the better. Poland's economy grew at a rate of more than 4 percent a year, far more than any of its neighbors. That meant that people had more money to spend on cars, video games, refrigerators, and other consumer goods.

The newly built PGE Arena in Gdańsk, a city in northern Poland, is one of several new soccer stadiums that reflect Poland's prosperity.

All that spending helped Poland survive the world financial crisis that began in 2008. While other countries, such as Greece, teetered on the edge of bankruptcy, Poland's economy hummed. New construction of a soccer stadium and shopping malls shows Poland's prosperity. That prosperity is allowing Poland, with Ukraine, to host the 2012 European Soccer Championship. Four Polish cities have improved their infrastructure and built or improved stadiums for the matches and camps for the thousands of soccer fans who will attend.

For Americans and many others, Poland has been a land of opportunity. The country has an appetite for foreign products, and the cost for running a business in Poland is low. "To have someone working for you in the States, it's at least $10 an hour (about $1,600 a month). In Poland, it's about $300 a month," says Magdalena Zucca.

Poland faces problems that often result from globalization. Its traditions are changing, and new ways of life are emerging. Yet partly due to globalization, the country has also welcomed new opportunities that hold promise for the future.

Explore the Issue

1. **Analyze Effects** How has globalization helped and hurt the Polish people? What is one example of a benefit and an example of a drawback?

2. **Make Inferences** Why is the European Union an example of globalization?

The PGE Arena holds 47,000 people and will be one of the arenas used for the 2012 Euro Soccer Championship, hosted by Poland and Ukraine.

China's New
GLOBAL
ECONOM

BIRTH OF A MIDDLE CLASS

Eric Wang is the face of the new middle class in China today. He buys coffee from a well-known American coffee shop and sips it as he travels to work. The firm where Eric works helps international companies get on the stock exchange in Beijing. While his family still lives as peasants on a rice farm, he has an apartment in the city and makes good money working with foreign businesses.

Eric knows how lucky he is. Thirty years ago China had a very small **middle class**, which is the social group between rich and poor. No foreign businesses were allowed, and Eric's current profession did not exist in China. He still returns to help work on the farm in the summers and does not forget his roots. "I'm lucky, but others have similar stories," says Wang. "It's a trend."

A large middle class in China is a boon for everyone. It means that millions of Chinese will become consumers of goods made both in China and around the world. Being middle class means that Chinese can spend money on goods not needed for survival, such as cars, electronics, and fashionable clothing.

FACTORY WORKERS AND ROBOTS

The trend is not true for everyone. Millions work like Ma Li Qun in low-paying jobs assembling high-priced electronics for American and Japanese companies. Working each day on the assembly line isn't just dull, but stressful. "We were not allowed to talk," Ma Li says. "We weren't even allowed to look around."

Still, Ma Li works, not wanting to lose his only source of income. His employer plans to replace most of its employees with 1 million robots, sometimes called "bots." Unlike humans, bots are more productive and don't need to be paid. Ma Li hopes his job is safe.

Such is life in modern China, where 30 years of rapid growth have transformed the country into the world's second largest economy. By 2030, China's middle class will be four times larger than the middle class in the United States. However, all Chinese do not share in the new prosperity.

This car factory in east China, operated by workers and robots, shows the increasing purchasing power of China's middle class.

UNDER MAO'S THUMB

China has gone through many changes in its long history. In 1949 the communists, led by their leader Mao Zedong (MOW zee-DAHNG), took over the government. The government owned or controlled most of the economic activities in the country.

At that time China had very little industry. Mao hoped to compete with the world's richest countries by building more bridges, better farms, and more machines. China was closed to the outside world. The government strictly controlled all people's work and lives. No one could own property, and millions lived in poverty. Mao's plan turned out to be an economic disaster.

After Mao's death in 1976, China began moving toward an economy that is still centrally planned but allows more free enterprise. China now permits individuals to own private property. However, the Chinese government still owns many companies, and it guides the direction of the economy. For example, the government is funding the construction of bullet trains. Since the early 1980s, China has strengthened its economy by building up its businesses, factories, and military. It now exports products to countries around the world.

HUMMING ALONG

With these changes, China has prospered. The country's economy has exploded, creating a large middle class. Today, although many Chinese make more money than ever, most workers' wages are still well below what workers in other countries earn.

Such cheap labor allows China to keep prices down and to sell more products. Those inexpensive goods have improved the lives of many Chinese and the lives of people in other countries, including the United States. At the same time, businesses in other countries have had a hard time competing with China's products. Higher wages and expenses mean others cannot make the products as cheaply as the Chinese do.

Exporting products isn't the only thing that keeps China's economy very active. The Chinese have a huge appetite for corn, oil, copper, aluminum, and other products, which they import. In addition, globalization has allowed China to rebuild its roads, bridges, and dams.

Chinese teens play laser tag at a Fun Fair in Hong Kong. Their new freedoms reflect Western culture.

A Chinese businessman talks on his cell phone in downtown Shanghai. Shanghai is a key city for international trade.

China has developed bullet trains that speed upwards of 125 mph to provide better and faster transportation. Such high-speed technology contrasts with the lives of traditional farmers.

NEW CITIES AND FASHIONS

Nothing shows China's success more than its skyscrapers, subways, and super-fast bullet trains. Since it emerged as a global power, China's cities have gone on a building binge. For example, in Wuhan, workers are building a new subway with nearly 140 miles of track. The subway is part of a $120 billion construction project that includes two airport terminals and a huge office tower.

Young people especially are enjoying China's wealth. In the 1970s, under Mao, young Chinese wore drab military clothing. Today, they wear Western-style clothing. "Fashion is one area where young Chinese feel they can be totally free," says fashion editor Nels Frye.

CHINA'S OTHER SIDE

Still, not everyone is doing well, especially in rural areas. In farming regions, more than 57 million poor people live on less than $10 per month. Many do not have clean water, electricity, or paved roads. Poorly paid factory workers such as Ma Li Qun wait to see if robots will take their jobs.

The environment has also been hurt badly as the economy grows. Factories have fouled the air and polluted the water. Sun Haixia (SUHN hy-SHAH), walking to a hospital in Lifen, sees the impact of globalization daily. Toxic smoke and soot from China's coal industry cause people on the street to wear masks. "We've pushed our environment to its limits," Sun says.

Globalization has brought huge benefits to China—and great challenges. The country's environmental problems are serious, and the gap between wealthy and poor has been growing. Yet, in recent years, the government has begun to take steps to lower the pollution. It has, for example, started to build water-treatment plants. These steps are a sign that the country recognizes problems that rapid economic growth has created.

Explore the Issue

1. **Identify Causes** What changes since the 1970s have made China's economy a success?

2. **Identify Effects** What are two ways in which China's emergence as a global power has hurt the country?

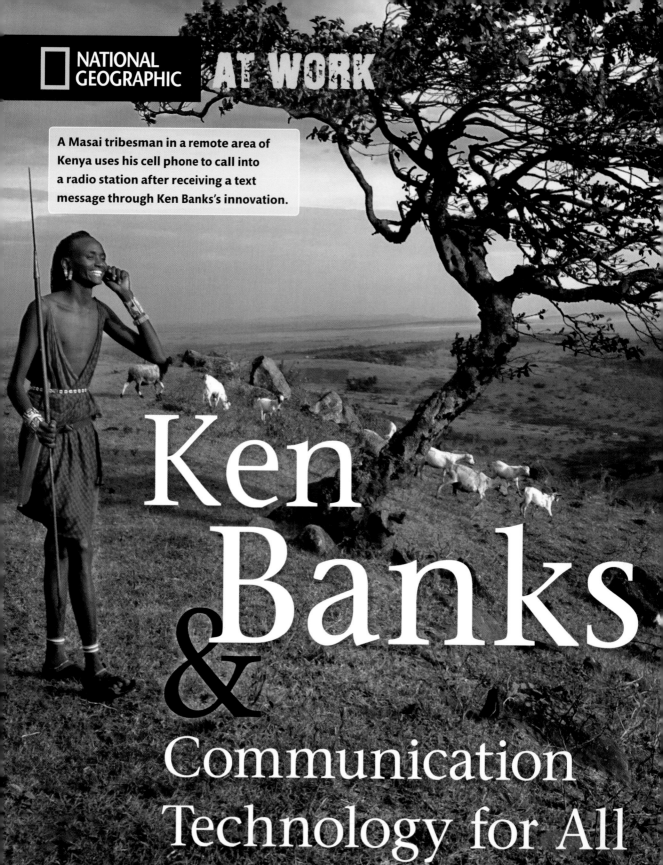

A Masai tribesman in a remote area of Kenya uses his cell phone to call into a radio station after receiving a text message through Ken Banks's innovation.

Ken Banks
& Communication Technology for All

WHAT DID YOU SAY?

Globalization helps people around the world communicate with one another. That's the insight that Ken Banks had as he thought about how to help people living far away from cities in South Africa, Cambodia, and throughout the world.

When the rains come to the remote Cambodian village of Ta Reach, Sophana Pich (suh-FAN-nuh PIK) gets to work helping people with malaria, a deadly disease carried by rain-loving mosquitoes. In Ta Reach, Sophana usually diagnoses five to six cases each month. Not long ago, it took time for Sophana to communicate with doctors in Cambodia's capital, Phnom Penh (puh-NAHM PEN), about 93 miles away. There are no phone lines and no Internet connecting Ta Reach to the capital. The delay meant that help could not arrive in time.

Ken Banks, a National Geographic Emerging Explorer, saw the same problem in South Africa. Today, thanks to a computer software program that Banks introduced, health care workers can communicate quickly. "Before, it would take a month before this information was reported," Sophana says.

LINKING ACROSS LONG DISTANCES

We all take talking to our friends for granted. Some of us use cell phones, others text or tweet, and still others send e-mails. However, in many rural areas, such communication is impossible. No one knows this better than Ken Banks.

When he was working in South Africa, Banks saw that people could not communicate over long distances. Parts of South Africa had no Internet service. Most of the phones in use across Africa today are very basic; they could not support the Internet even if there were Internet service. Banks wanted to find a way to allow people in these areas to talk to others far away. One day as he sat at home watching a soccer game, Banks had an idea: what would happen if he built a system that used a cell phone network instead of the Internet?

The result was a computer program called FrontlineSMS, which turns a cheap laptop and a cell phone into a text messaging communication center that does not require Internet access.

Ken Banks got the inspiration for FrontlineSMS while in South Africa.

A village phone operator in Uganda shows off her cell phone, which she hires out for use one call or text at a time.

"Anyone can use this tool to solve a problem they see in the place where they live." —Ken Banks

TWO STEPS TO COMMUNICATION

How does FrontlineSMS work? First, the users download the free software. Then they simply attach a cable from the mobile phone to the computer. All that people need is one bar of mobile phone coverage to send their message and communicate with anyone on a contact list, no matter how far away the other person is. "After downloading the free software online, you never need the Internet again," Banks says.

Banks's software has helped millions of people around the world. It saves time and lives. In Cambodia, Sophana and others use FrontlineSMS to report cases of malaria instantly to the government. The message includes the patient's name, age, location, and symptoms of illness. The government can respond to problems right away.

People living in the African country of Malawi began receiving better health care when a college student brought hundreds of recycled phones and a laptop loaded with the FrontlineSMS.

"ALL I HAD WAS AN IDEA"

Banks is a scientist trained in social anthropology, the study of how people live. He also works in **conservation**, or efforts to save the environment. However, computer technology really excites Banks. Because of his new system, rural areas can get medicine. Doctors can treat patients who are hundreds of miles away. Farmers can find out current crop prices.

Beyond medicine and farming, Banks's system also helps people troubleshoot other technology problems in Africa. For example, he helped develop and share ways to get rid of kitchen waste using biogas digestors.

"Anyone can use this tool to solve a problem they see in the place where they live," Banks says. "We need to help people realize that if you care enough, you can do meaningful things without piles of money or expensive hardware. All I had was an idea."

Explore the Issue

1. **Identify Problems** Why couldn't people in remote regions communicate over long distances?

2. **Identify Solutions** How does Banks's tool solve communication problems in remote areas?

What Can I DO?

Catalog Where Products Are Made—and become a knowledgeable consumer

Your athletic shoes, computer, and smartphone were probably made somewhere other than the United States. Do you know where they were made? Research and catalog where different brands of the same product came from and share what you've learned with your class. You and your classmates will then become knowledgeable consumers.

IDENTIFY

- Pick any manufactured product, such as athletic shoes, televisions, or smartphones.

- Choose five brand names for that product on which to base your research on competing products.

- Create a simple database or spreadsheet to record the information from your research.

ORGANIZE

- Use the Internet and the library to find where each brand was made.

- Trace and identify how each product arrived in the United States.

- Develop a list of questions that you can use to learn more about the path the product followed.

- Interview a store owner, manager, or clerk to see how each product arrived in the store.

These jeans took a long path through several countries to get to the consumer.

DOCUMENT

- Take your own photos or download photos of each brand of the product.

- Identify the countries that contributed parts of each brand and the country where each product was assembled.

- Write a description comparing and contrasting where each brand was made and how it came to the United States.

- Compare the costs of the different brands.

SHARE

- Create a map or a chart with arrows showing the route each brand took on its journey to the United States.

- Present to your classmates each of the products' country of origin, how it was made, and how it got to the store. Persuade classmates to consider where and how each brand was made before buying.

Write an
Argumentative Article

How do consumers make buying choices? Should Americans buy products that are "Made in America"? Write a paper arguing for or against a public awareness campaign to persuade Americans to purchase products made in the United States.

RESEARCH

Use the Internet, books, magazines, and newspapers to find support for your point of view. Make sure your sources are reliable. Look for the following:

- Several reasons that support your argument
- Costs or economic statistics that support your opinion
- Quotations and facts that support your opinion

As you do your research, be sure to take notes on note cards or on a computer.

DRAFT

Write the first draft of the article. It should be four paragraphs long.

- The first paragraph, or introduction, should introduce your opinion about the value of a public campaign to "buy American."
- The following two paragraphs should develop your argument with clear reasons, relevant facts, definitions, and solid, effective details. Use direct quotations or paraphrase the information and conclusions of others, such as economists, consumers, or sellers.
- In the fourth paragraph, provide a conclusion that reinforces your argument for or against the campaign.

REVISE & EDIT

Look over your draft to make sure your argument is clearly stated and supported by the evidence.

- Does the introduction state your opinion in an interesting way?
- Did you include convincing, relevant facts?
- Are the supporting paragraphs focused on sound logic and quotations from knowledgeable people?

Revise the article to make it as persuasive as possible.

- Use transition words and phrases, along with strong verbs, to make your writing interesting, lively, and convincing.
- Make sure the quotations are accurate and the information is correct.

Proofread your paper for spelling and punctuation.

PUBLISH & PRESENT

Combine your article with an article from a classmate who took the opposite point of view. Staple the articles together, create a cover for the published document, and copy it for your class. Have your classmates read the document and vote on which article is more persuasive.

economy

natural resource

Common Market *n.*, an economic alliance of countries in the European Union that dropped trade barriers among its members

communist *n.*, a person who believes in communism, a social and economic philosophy marked by a classless society and the absence of private property

conservation *n.*, an effort to protect the environment

democratic *adj.*, having a government in which power is in the hands of the people and exercised by their representatives

economy *n.*, a system of producing and distributing wealth

European Union (EU) *n.*, an economic and political association of countries in Europe

free enterprise *n.*, an economic system in which private businesses organize and operate for profit competitively, with a minimum of government interference

globalization *n.*, the way countries use technology, communication, and transportation to connect with each other

middle class *n.*, an economic and social class between rich and poor

natural resource *n.*, a valuable material that comes from the environment, such as coal, oil, or gold

conservation

European Union

W E
S

SWEDEN FINLAND

ESTONIA

LATVIA

North DENMARK
Sea

Baltic Sea

LITHUANIA

IRELAND

GREAT
BRITAIN

NETHERLANDS

ATLANTIC
OCEAN

BELGIUM GERMANY POLAND

LUXEMBOURG

CZECH
REPUBLIC

SLOVAKIA

FRANCE

AUSTRIA HUNGARY

SLOVENIA ROMANIA

PORTUGAL SPAIN

ITALY

BULGARIA

Mediterranean Sea

GREECE

Bla

CYPR

globalization

INDEX

SKILLS